LEARNING ABOUT
Insects

Catherine Veitch

The author would like to dedicate this book to her mother,
Jacqueline Veitch, who inspired her with a love of nature.

Raintree is an imprint of Capstone Global Library Limited, a company incorporated in England and Wales having its registered office at 7 Pilgrim Street, London, EC4V 6LB – Registered company number: 6695582

To contact Raintree:
Phone: 0845 6044371
Fax: + 44 (0) 1865 312263
Email: myorders@raintreepublishers.co.uk
Outside the UK please telephone +44 1865 312262.

Text © Capstone Global Library Limited 2014
First published in hardback in 2014
The moral rights of the proprietor have been asserted.

Edited by Dan Nunn, Rebecca Rissman, and Sian Smith
Designed by Joanna Hinton-Malivoire
Picture research by Mica Brancic
Production by Sophia Argyris
Originated by Capstone Global Library Ltd
Printed and bound in China by South China Printing Company Ltd

ISBN 978 1 406 26610 8
17 16 15 14 13
10 9 8 7 6 5 4 3 2 1

British Library Cataloguing in Publication Data
A catalogue record for this book is available from the British Library.

Acknowledgements

We would like to thank Michael Bright for his invaluable help in the preparation of this book.

We would also like to thank the following for permission to reproduce photographs: Science Photo Library p.11 (Visuals Unlimited, Inc./Terry Priest); Shutterstock pp.4 (© Andrey Pavlov), 5 (© Karel Gallas), 6 (© Vladimir Konjushenko), 7 (© Christian Musat), 8 (© Anson0618), 9 (© PetrP), 10 (© alslutsky), 12 (© Cosmin Manci), 13 (© Erkki Alvenmod), 14 (© Palto), 15 (© Henrik Larsson), 16 (© ajt), 17 (© optimarc), 18 inset (© liou.zojan), 18 main (© Eric Isselee), 19 (© D. Kucharski& K. Kucharska), 20 (© Suede Chen), 21 (© erni), 21 (© Biehler Michael), 22 antenna (© ajt), 22 claw (© efendy), 22 jaw (© Karel Gallas), 22 proboscis (© Christian Musat), 23 spine (© Eric Isselee), 23 sting (© Biehler Michael), 23 wingcase (© Palto), 23 wings (© alslutsky).

Front cover photograph of a dragonfly reproduced with permission of Shutterstock (© Rob Hainer). Back cover photograph of a ladybird reproduced with permission of Shutterstock (© Palto).

Every effort has been made to contact copyright holders of material reproduced in this book. Any omissions will be rectified in subsequent printings if notice is given to the publisher.

Contents

Ant

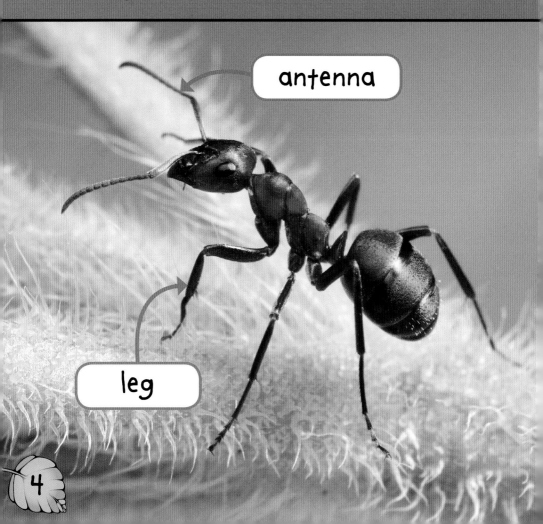

antenna

leg

4

Beetle

jaws

wing case

Bumblebee

wing

body

Butterfly

proboscis

wing

Cockroach

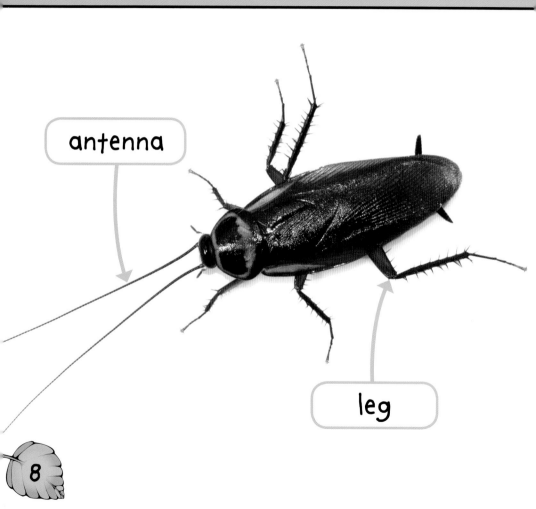

antenna

leg

Cricket

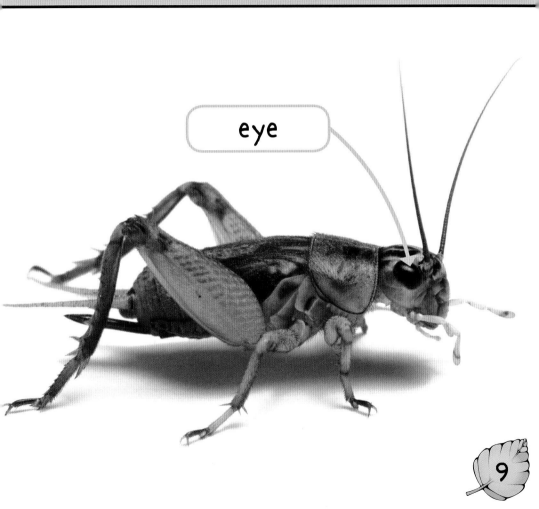

eye

9

wing

body

Firefly

antenna

wing case

wing

Flea

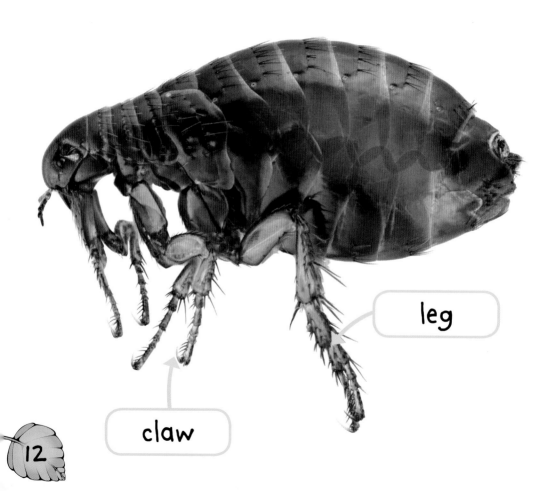

leg

claw

Fly

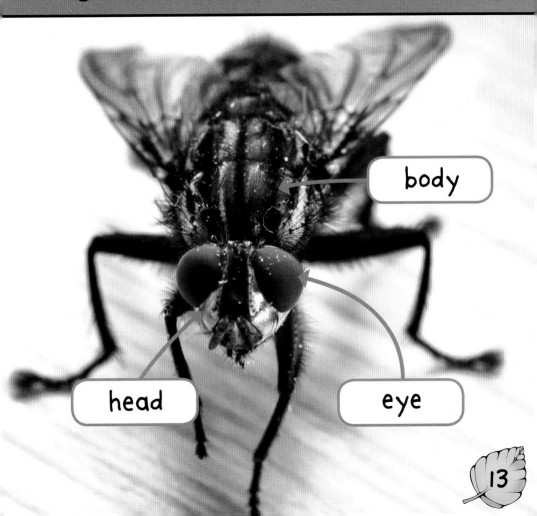

body

head

eye

13

Ladybird

wing case

antenna

14

Mosquito

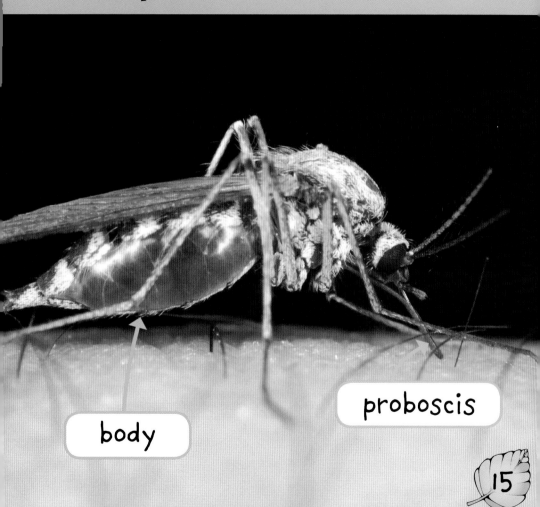

body

proboscis

15

Moth

antenna

wing

16

Pond skater

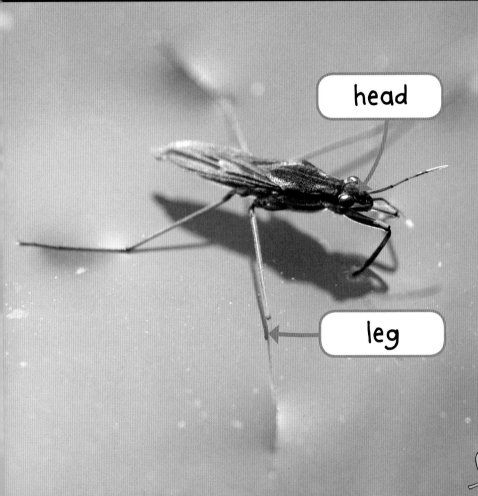

head

leg

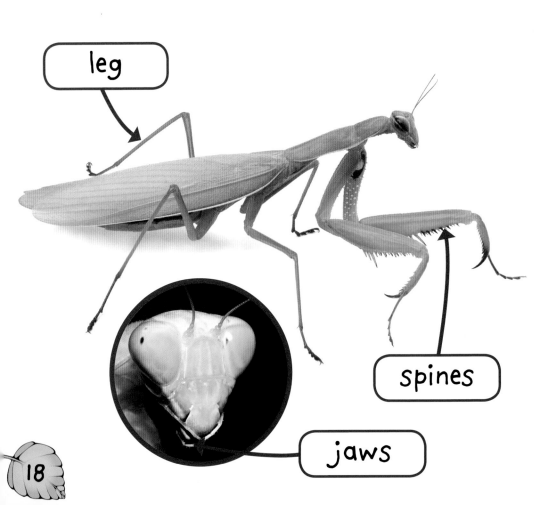

leg

spines

jaws

Silverfish

antenna

leg

19

Stinkbug

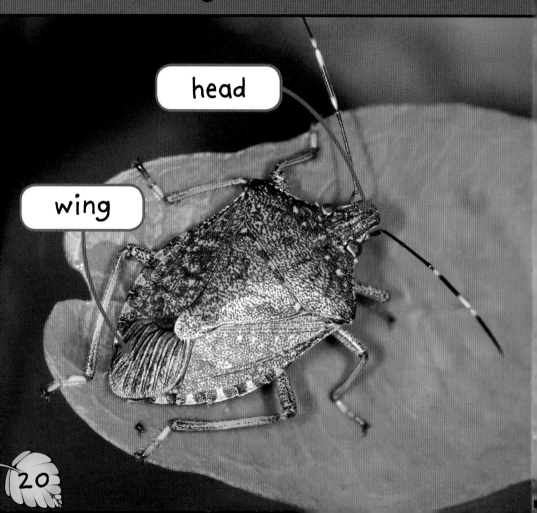

head

wing

Wasp

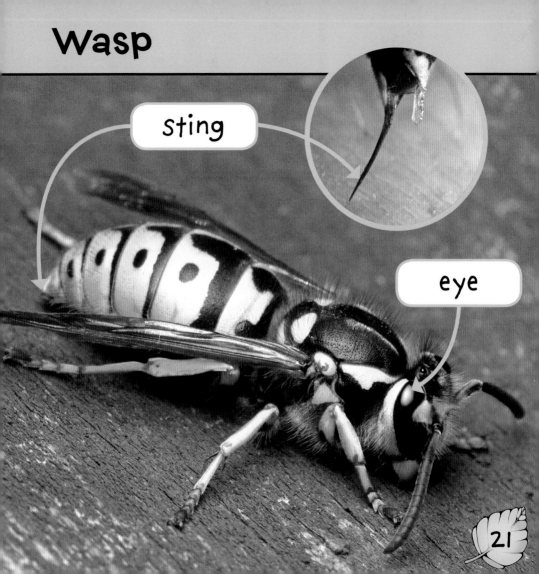

sting

eye

Picture glossary

antenna long, thin feeler on the head of an insect. Insects use antennae to sense the world around them.

claw long, pointed part on the end of an insect's leg. Insects use claws to hold on to things.

jaws an insect's mouth and teeth. Some insects, such as stag beetles, have special jaws that stick out.

proboscis long, pointed part of an insect's mouth that can be used for sucking up food

22

 **spines** stiff spikes. Insects use spines to help them climb, grip on to things, or to keep them safe from enemies.

 **sting** part of an insect that can prick an animal and cause pain. Insects can use stingers to frighten other animals away.

 **wing case** hard covering that protects an insect's wings

 **wings** parts on the bodies of some insects. Insects use their wings to fly.

- Go on a nature walk with the children. Take this book along, and ask the children to spot some of the insects in the book. Can they point to the different insect parts, such as antennae, wings, and legs?

- Ask children to sketch or photograph what they see. Can they label the insects and insect parts? Use the pictures and labels to make a book.

- Discuss the different body parts of insects and what the insects might use them for. Look at the ant on page 4. What do the children think the ant uses its antennae for? Explain that all insects have a pair of antennae, usually near their eyes, though some can be small and hard to spot. Different insects can do different things with their antennae, but they all use antennae to sense the world around them. Like many other insects, ants use their antennae to smell, taste, and touch with. An ant can even use its antennae to tap another ant on the head to ask it to share its food.

24